This slice of vegan heaven is dedicated to our family, who infused spice into our lives with a sprinkle of wonderment, a dash of creativity, and a heaping spoonful of grit and determination.
Xoxo- Victor & Mika

Chasing Vegan: Making Vegan Fun
Victor & Mika's Story

We were not born vegan.

Victor and I did not start our journeys devouring plant-based meals. In fact, it was quite the opposite. Our diverse families thoroughly enjoyed our cultural delicacies with a whole-hearted enthusiasm.

Victor was born into a vibrant family of Mexican Heritage that celebrated their meals with flavor-infused cultural staples such as enchiladas, Arroz Con Pollo, tamales, and cinnamon-dusted churros. His fondest memories are of his grandmother, staking claim to her modest kitchen as the queen of her domain. He remembers watching her skillfully maneuver her knife as she diced onion after onion. The cadence of her knife slicing jalapenos was the backdrop to many conversations, and some of the most precious moments he shared with his grandmother. These meals created memories that seared themselves into Victor's DNA.

I was also born into an unabashedly, rich cultural heritage. As the daughter of Haitian immigrants, our food connected us to our family roots. Akin to the country's language, Haitian food has a sense of the blended influences of Crèole. A combination of spices—basic yet zippy—grounded in the reality of the tropics, and accompanied by the back-story of African heritage touched with a hint of French complexity, are the foundations of my culture's epicurean palate.

I watched mama toil for hours in the kitchen, and I wondered why she spent so much time chopping and dicing and measuring. It seemed so laborious. Like a thankless task that resulted in her brood of children gulping down their meals and promptly excusing themselves from the table to run-off to their activities. "Mama," I would ask, "Why do you spend so much time preparing these meals when everyone eats and runs?" My mama wiped her hands on her tea towel, pulled back the tattered kitchen chair, and sat down. She looked me in the eyes. Her inquisitive gaze locked with mine, and she took a deep breath. "Mika, my darling," she held out her hand and grabbed mine. "I chop and dice and bake and fry because the food on this table is love." That was the moment that I understood the power food had to be an extension of love. Victor tells me stories of how his grandmother and mother also poured their hearts into their culinary creations. When Victor and I united as a team, we expressed our love through the food we prepared. Now, we have the opportunity to share this intimate expression with you.

So, how did we choose vegan? Let me start by saying, I did not choose a vegan lifestyle, but rather, the vegan lifestyle chose me. Vegan was never on my radar. I was a fast-food enthusiast, so my front seat often contained greasy cheeseburger remnants. I made my rounds through drive-thrus and devoured right-out-of-the-fryer french fries. "Extra salt, please!" I would holler to the server in the window. The acid-burning unnatural nectar of Coke washed down these meals as I raced to my next appointment. I repeated this ritual daily.

As I indulged in the fast-paced life of being a celebrity stylist, I began to feel fatigued and uncomfortable. This was not a "my jeans-are-getting-too-tight uncomfortable." This was a steady cadence of tummy aches, bloating, and sharp twinges in my abdomen. When the swelling and pain became unbearable, I forced myself to see a doctor.

The memory of being ushered into a sterile, beige room, cloaked in a paper dress as I waited for the doctor to enter, is seared in my psyche. I'm naturally optimistic, so I believed with all of my heart that everything would be okay. As I mustered all of the positive thoughts possible, my heart sank as my eyes met with my physician. He was forthright in his diagnosis. At this point, my optimistic lens on the world became clouded with confusion and fear.

"Ms. Altidor," the doctor began as he scanned his chart, "You have several tumors growing on the outside of your uterus, and they are large." *Ding! Ding! Ding!* No wonder I appeared six months pregnant! My mind raced—*I can get some antibiotics, and soon, this health disaster will be a distant memory.*

I met with words such as "hysterectomy" and "surgical procedure." The physician assured me that he could remove these fast-growing tumors through medical intervention. I ran out of that office, scared, in pain, and devastated. I knew I had to change everything about my lifestyle.

Fast-Forward two years. After months of researching this particular kind of tumor, I realized the hormones of meat-based products were their lifeblood. I slowly eased into the vegan lifestyle and ultimately embraced it. My tumors began to shrink, the pain eased, and I felt in control of my health again.

When I met Victor in late 2015, I was an enthusiastic supporter of all things plant-based. My love, Victor, met me with resistance. Remember, he is of Mexican Heritage, and meat is a mainstay at every meal. I never pushed veganism on him—or anyone else for that matter. However, one day he surprised me. Victor explained that he had been doing independent research on the health benefits of a vegan diet. He told me that he planned to give up meat and their bi-products. This proud carnivorous Latino man was going to stand by my side in living a healthier life.

Victor and I were never chasing a lifestyle. We were simply searching for a quality of life that would allow us to live our delicious purpose and accelerate our dreams. This newfound energy sparked us into training to be world-class pastry chefs. This led to our distinguished reputation of being the only Vegan Bakery in Polk County, Florida. With each wedding cake we design and each catering event we execute, we share our passion with you. Each recipe is an extension of our love and our vision to empower individuals to stop chasing and start being.

We hope that you can live a decadent life and not miss out on the flavor.

Xoxo- Mika and Victor

Table of Contents

Cakes

Toppings

Cupcakes

Muffins and Breads

○ ● ○ *◇ * ◆ * ◇ * ○ ● ○

Ingredient Guide

FLOURS

All-Purpose Flour: This basic flour is a pantry staple and can be used in most baked goods.

Bread Flour: This flour is super-high in gluten and perfect for yeasted bread.

Gluten-Free Flours: There are a variety of gluten-free flours available. They are made from various grains, nuts, and starches.

SUGARS

Sugar: Plain white sugar is refined from sugar cane or beets.

Brown Sugar, Light or Dark: This soft, earthy-tasting sugar is white sugar flavored with molasses. If the sugar hardens, leave a slice of apple or a piece of bread in the container for a few hours overnight.

Decorating or Coarse Sugar: The granules are about four times larger than granulated sugar, available in many colors, and great for decorating.

Agave Nectar: Made from the sap of the same plant that produces tequila, it tastes similar to honey.

LEAVENERS

Baking Soda: Also known as sodium bicarbonate or bicarbonate of soda. Baking soda is used as a chemical leavener to make dough and batter rise.

Baking Powder: This leavener is composed of baking soda, an acid (usually cream of tartar), and a moisture absorber, like cornstarch.

Active Dry Yeast: This is a yeast that has been dehydrated into tiny granules. Before using, it must be reactivated or "bloomed" by being mixed with warm water (about 110℉) and sometimes a small amount of sugar for the yeast to feed on.

Instant Yeast: Also called "quick rise," "rapid rise," or "fast rise" yeast. Produced similar to active dry yeast, it has more porous granules that don't require the reactivation step.

PLANT MILK

Plant milk is a dairy-free alternative and made from plants. The most common options are:

- Almond milk
- Rice milk
- Coconut milk
- Oats milk
- Hemp milk
- Flax milk
- Macadamia nut milk
- Cashew milk

CHOCOLATES

Unsweetened Chocolate: This is also called baking chocolate and, as the name implies, doesn't have any added sugar.

Dark Chocolate: Dark chocolate can be called bittersweet or semisweet. Bittersweet chocolate is less sweet than semisweet.

White Chocolate: This is not chocolate because it does not contain chocolate liquor. However, it contains cocoa butter, sugar, vanilla, and lecithin.

Chocolate Chips: These contain less cocoa butter than chocolate, which is why they can retain their shape when baked. It is best to use these where you want the chocolate-chip shape. Store tightly wrapped.

Unsweetened Cocoa Powder: Cocoa powder is made when cocoa butter is removed from the chocolate liquor. It is cacao beans that have been fermented, dried, roasted, shelled, and ground into a paste.

OTHER INGREDIENTS

Plant Butter: Dairy-free alternatives derived from plants. Common brands:

- Earth Balance
- Miyoko's Kitchen
- Wayfare Whipped
- I Can't Believe It's Not Butter
- Betty Crocker Plant Butter

Buttermilk: It is a dairy-free alternative made from mixing a cup of plant milk with 1 tablespoon of vinegar.

Coconut Cream: It is much thicker and richer than coconut milk. Made from simmering four parts shredded coconut in one part water, it is a plant-based version of heavy cream that is perfect for whipping due to its high-fat content.

Psyllium Husk Powder: It is used to retain moisture and help bread from becoming too crumbly.

Vanilla Extract: A must-have pantry item. For the best flavor, use pure vanilla extract, but artificial can be used in a pinch.

Salt: Most baking recipes are written for a fine-grain salt unless otherwise specified.

Himalayan Salt: This comes from pink salt rock in Pakistan near the Himalayas and is rich in nutrients.

○●○●○●○●○○●○○●○●○●○●○●○●●

Pro Tips

Dry Ingredients: Sifted dry ingredients are lighter and easier to mix with other ingredients. This process helps to get rid of lumps.

Wet ingredients: Wet ingredients are best kept at room temperature unless the recipe specifies otherwise.

Equipment & Tools

Oven Preheat lets you bake faster, giving the oven time to reach the ideal temperature.

Oven Thermometer ensures your baked goods are baking at the right temperature.

Kitchen Scales are the best way to measure accurately and get great results.

A **whisk** is a great tool to mix dry or wet ingredients in a mixing bowl quickly.

A **Cookie/Ice Cream Scoop** is the secret to getting the same sized cookies.

<u>Vegan Carrot Cake</u>

This is our favorite go-to recipe. It is rich, complex, and simple to assemble. Serve it to guests or that someone special. They don't even have to be vegan—after one bite, they will be asking for more!

Serving Size: 10

Ingredients:

1⅓ cups all-purpose flour
1½ teaspoons baking soda
½ teaspoon salt
½ teaspoon baking powder
1 teaspoon cinnamon
½ teaspoon ground ginger
1⅓ cups sugar
⅔ cup oil
⅔ cup apple sauce
1 tablespoon vanilla
⅓ cup crushed drained pineapples
2 cups grated carrot
½ cup chopped walnuts (optional)

Instructions:

1. Preheat the oven to 350°F, and grease cake pans. (Tip: I use two 7-inch pans)

2. Combine all wet ingredients—sugar, oil, applesauce, crushed pineapples, and vanilla extract in a mixing bowl and mix.

3. In a separate bowl, mix the flour, baking soda, baking powder, salt, ginger, and cinnamon.

4. Add the dry to the wet and mix well.

5. Add walnuts (optional). Fold in carrots and mix until well combined.

6. Pour batter into your cake pans and bake for 25-30 mins, until a toothpick poked into the center comes out clean. (Tip: Your oven may bake faster or slower, keep an eye on your cakes)

7. Remove from the oven and let the cake cool completely on a wire rack.

8. Once cooled, frost.

Best Chocolate Cake Ever

We originally made this cake for a little boy's birthday party. His vegan grandmother was hosting the party and wanted it to be perfect. The guest of honor was not vegan, and Grandma was concerned that he would frown when he took one bite into a celery-tasting, dry vegan pastry. This little boy did the opposite. He took one forkful, smiled, and declared that it was "all his" and he would not allow anyone else to eat it.

Serving Size: 10

Ingredients:

2 cups all-purpose flour

2 cups of sugar

¾ cup unsweetened cocoa powder

2 teaspoons baking powder

1½ teaspoons baking soda

1 teaspoon salt

1 teaspoon instant coffee

1 cup plant milk

1 teaspoon apple cider vinegar

½ cup oil

2 teaspoons vanilla

1 cup boiling water

Instructions:

1. Preheat the oven to 350ºF.

2. Prepare two 9-inch cake pans by spraying with baking spray or buttering and lightly flouring.

3. In a mixing bowl, combine and whisk apple cider vinegar and plant milk and set aside 10 minutes to churn. This is our vegan buttermilk.

4. Add flour, sugar, cocoa, baking powder, baking soda, salt, and coffee to a large bowl or the bowl of a stand mixer. Whisk through to combine or, using your paddle attachment, stir through flour mixture until well combined.

5. Add oil, buttermilk, and vanilla to the flour mixture and mix on medium speed until well combined.

6. Reduce speed and carefully add boiling water to the cake batter until well combined.

7. Distribute cake batter evenly between the two prepared cake pans.

8. Bake for 30-35 minutes, until a toothpick in the middle of the chocolate cake comes out clean.

Continued on next page

Best Chocolate Cake Ever - Continued from the previous page

9. Remove from the oven and cool for about 10 minutes.

10. Remove from the pan and cool completely. (Tip: resist the temptation to nibble)

11. Frost cake with Chocolate Buttercream Frosting.

WHY
plant-based

- IT REDUCES AND CAN REVERSE CHRONIC DISEASE

- IT CONSERVES WATER

- IT LOWERS GREEN-HOUSE EMISSIONS

- IT CONSERVES LAND

- IT HELPS REDUCE SPECIES EXTINCTION
-
- IT REDUCES WASTE POLLUTION

- IT SLOWS DEFORESTATION

- IT BOOSTS ATHLETIC PERFORMANCE

- IT HELPS ALLIVIATE WORLD HUNGER

Red Velvet Cake

This decadent cake melts in your mouth with each bite. No exaggeration—It melts on the tongue. It is mellow yet rich in flavor and perfect for any celebration.

Serving Size: 10

○●○●○●○●○●○○●○●○○●○●○○●○○●○●○

Ingredients:

2 cups all-purpose flour

1 teaspoon baking soda

½ teaspoon salt

1 tablespoon cocoa powder (unsweetened)

1 cup milk

1 tablespoon white vinegar

1 cup of sugar

2 teaspoons vanilla extract

⅓ cup oil

2¾ tablespoons vegan red food dye

Instructions:

1. Preheat the oven to 350ºF.

2. In a mixing bowl, combine and whisk apple cider vinegar and plant milk. Set aside for 10 minutes. It will curdle and turn into buttermilk.

3. In a mixing bowl, combine and mix the flour, sugar, baking soda, salt, and cocoa powder.

4. Add the buttermilk, vanilla extract, oil, vinegar, and red food dye into the mixing bowl and mix. (Tip: Use a hand whisk to get rid of any lumps)

5. Grease two 7-inch cake pans with oil spray and divide the batter evenly between them.

6. Tap cake pans on the counter 2-3 times to gently release air pockets for even baking.

7. Place into the oven and bake for 30 minutes.

8. After 30 minutes, insert a toothpick into the center of the cake, and if it comes out clean, it is cooked.

9. Let the cakes cool on a cooling rack completely before frosting.

○●○●○●○○●○●○●○●○●○○●○

Vanilla Cake

This moist cake is versatile and goes with everything. Top it with our creamy buttercream frosting and decorate it with chocolate shavings or colorful rosettes.

Serving Size: 10

Ingredients:

1 cup plant milk
1 tablespoon apple cider or white vinegar
½ cup oil
1 tablespoon vanilla
1¾ cups sugar
3 cups flour
1 tablespoon baking powder
½ teaspoon salt

Instructions:

1. Preheat the oven to 350ºF.

2. Grease two 8-inch pans.

3. Combine and whisk vinegar and plant milk in a mixing bowl. This becomes the buttermilk.

4. In a separate mixing bowl, combine all the dry ingredients, whisk, and set aside.

5. Add oil and vanilla to the vegan buttermilk and mix until well combined. Then add dry ingredients to the wet ingredients and mix until well combined.

6. Divide batter evenly in two greased 8-inch cake pans.

7. Tap cake pans on the counter table 2-3 times gently to release air pockets for even baking.

8. Place into the oven and bake for 30 minutes.

9. After 30 minutes, insert a toothpick into the center of the cake, and if it comes out clean, it is cooked. (Tip: Let the cakes cool on a cooling rack completely before frosting)

Cream Cheese Frosting

Literally, the Icing on the Cake

Serving Size: 3 Cups

○●○●○●○●○●○●○●○●○●○●○●

Ingredients:

5 cups powdered sugar (Tip: Add more to taste)

1½ cups vegan butter

1 tablespoon lemon juice

3 tablespoons plant milk

1 tablespoon vanilla extract

1 tablespoon apple cider vinegar

Instructions:

1. Combine all ingredients in a food processor and process for about 1 minute. (Tip: Whisk by hand if you want to build muscle while you bake)

2. Scrape down the sides of the bowl and process until smooth.

3. Ice your cake.

◇◆*◇*◆*◇*◆*◇*◆*◇*◆*

○●○*◇*◆*◇*○●○

Chocolate Buttercream Frosting

Add a little something extra to your baked goods with this frosting recipe.

Serving Size: 3 Cups

Ingredients:

1 cup vegan butter softened to room temperature
¾ cup unsweetened cocoa powder
3½ cups powdered sugar
2 teaspoons pure vanilla extract
3 tablespoons unsweetened plant milk

Instructions:

1. Soften butter at room temperature for 15-30 minutes in a mixing bowl.

2. With a hand mixer or a stand mixer with a whisk attachment, beat the butter on medium speed for about 2 minutes.

3. Sift in the cocoa powder and powdered sugar, and add the vanilla and plant milk.

4. Beat on low speed for 30 seconds, then increase the speed to high and beat for 2-3 minutes, until combined and fluffy.

5. If the frosting is too thick, add another tablespoon of plant milk. If it is too thin, add an additional ¼ cup powdered sugar.

6. Frost your cake.

Vanilla Buttercream Frosting

You can frost anything and everything with this creamy concoction.

Serving Size: 3 Cups

○●○●○●○●○●○○●○●○●○●○○●○●●

Ingredients:
1 cup Earth Balance vegan butter, softened to room temperature
3 cups powdered sugar
2-3 tablespoons unsweetened non-dairy milk
1 teaspoon pure vanilla extract

Instructions:

1. Place the vegan butter in a mixing bowl and keep at room temperature for 20 minutes before beating with an electric mixer until creamy.

2. Gradually add the powdered sugar at a low mixing speed. Add vanilla.

3. Increase speed to medium. Add plant milk, 1 tablespoon at a time. (Tip: Check consistency after the second tablespoon of plant milk to see if a third tablespoon is needed) Beat for about 30 seconds until fluffy.

4. Ice your cake, cupcakes, or brownies.

○ ● ○ ● ○ ● ○ ● ○ ● ○ ● ○ ● ○ ● ○ ● ○ ● ○ ● ○ ● ○

Coconut Whipped Cream

This creamy topping adds a unique touch to any dessert.

Serving Size: 2 to 3 cups

Ingredients:

1 can coconut cream (chill overnight or longer)
6 tablespoons powdered sugar

Instructions:

1. Remove the can of coconut from the fridge, open it carefully. You will find that the cream has separated from the water and has risen to the top. Remove only the cream and place it in a mixing bowl, leaving the water in the can. (Tip: Save the coconut water to make smoothies or juices)

2. In your electric mixer, beat on low speed the coconut cream, gradually increasing the speed until the cream is whipped. Add the powdered sugar and whip again. (Tip: Do like the song says and "Whip it, Whip it good!")

3. Slather your treat in yumminess.

◇◆*◇*◆*◇*◆*◇*◆*◇*◆*◇*◆*

Victor & Mika's
Bakery

Vegan

Easy Chocolate Ganache

Thank Goodness that dairy-free ganache exists, and it is easy! Let us show you how.

Serving Size: 4 Cups

Ingredients:

1 tablespoon vegan butter

¾ cup coconut cream

1½ cups vegan dark chocolate chips

Instructions:

1. In a medium saucepan over medium heat, melt vegan butter.

2. Pour coconut cream and casually whisk with vegan butter. Let it simmer.

3. Remove the saucepan from heat and pour the chocolate into the coconut cream.

4. Whisk until well incorporated for 3-5 minutes. Chocolate chips will dissolve, and a dark shiny chocolate consistency will appear. It is ready to use for dipping, cake drips, candy molds, and so much more.

Lemon Cupcakes

These lemon cakes are a favorite at picnics. Pair with a fresh summer vegetable salad for the win!

Serving Size: 14 Cupcakes

Ingredients:

1⅔ cups all-purpose flour

1 cup of sugar

2 tablespoons lemon juice or the zest of two lemons

¼ teaspoon baking soda

1½ teaspoons baking powder

¼ teaspoon salt

¼ cup oil

1 teaspoon apple cider or white vinegar

½ cup vegan sour cream room temperature

¼ cup plant milk (warm)

¼ cup lemon juice

Instructions:

1. Preheat the oven to 350°F.

2. Place cupcake liners inside the cupcake pan.

3. Combine and whisk plant milk and vinegar to create buttermilk.

4. Sift the flour, baking soda, baking powder, and salt into a large bowl, then whisk together and set aside.

5. Add the sugar and lemon zest to a mixing bowl and whisk at high speed until well combined.

6. Combine the buttermilk, oil, lemon juice, sour cream, and sugar/lemon zest mixture to a medium bowl and whisk together.

7. Add the wet to the dry mixture and mix until just combined.

8. Fill cupcake liners about ¾ of the way.

9. Bake for 15-18 minutes. Insert a toothpick in the center of one cupcake. If the toothpick is clean, remove it from the oven and allow cupcakes to cool completely before frosting.

Oreo Cookie Cupcakes

When you can't decide between vanilla or chocolate—Choose both!

Serving Size: 12 Cupcakes

Ingredients:
1 cup plant milk
1 tablespoon apple cider or white vinegar
½ cup oil
1 tablespoon vanilla
1¾ cups sugar
3 cups flour
1 tablespoon baking powder
½ teaspoon salt
18-24 Oreos

Instructions:

1. Preheat the oven to 350ºF.

2. Place cupcake liners inside the cupcake pan.

3. Combine and whisk plant milk and vinegar to create buttermilk.

4. Sift the flour, baking soda, baking powder, and salt into a large bowl, then whisk together and set aside.

5. Add oil and vanilla to the vegan buttermilk and mix until well combined. Then add dry ingredients to the wet ingredients and mix until just combined. Crush 6 Oreos and fold into batter.

6. Fill cupcake liners about ¾ of the way. Then place an Oreo cookie inside each cupcake liner. Push the Oreo down until the batter covers it.

7. Bake for 15-18 minutes. Insert a toothpick in the center of one cupcake. If the toothpick is clean, remove it from the oven and allow cupcakes to cool completely before frosting.

8. Choose your favorite buttercream frosting—vanilla or chocolate—and garnish with an Oreo cookie on top.

Easy Blueberry Muffins

Loaded with flavorful blueberries, this classic muffin makes brunch extra special.

Serving Size: 12 Muffins

Ingredients:

1 cup all-purpose flour
½ cup whole wheat flour
1½ teaspoons baking soda
¼ teaspoon salt
½ cup melted butter
3 large ripe bananas mashed
½ cup of sugar
¼ cup dark brown sugar packed
¼ cup plant milk
1 tablespoon psyllium husk
1 teaspoon vanilla extract
¾ cup to 1 cup walnuts

Instructions:

1. Preheat the oven to 350°F.

2. Whisk dry ingredients, flour, baking soda, and salt together in a large mixing bowl. Set aside.

3. Melt butter. Set aside.

4. In a separate mixing bowl, mash bananas with a fork. Mix in butter, both sugars, plant milk, psyllium husk, and vanilla. Stir until well combined.

5. Combine wet ingredients into dry ingredients. Stir until just combined. (Tip: Do not over mix) Fold in half the walnuts.

6. Spoon batter evenly into 12 greased muffin cups. Then sprinkle the remainder of walnuts over top of muffins.

7. Bake for about 22 - 26 minutes or until muffins are golden brown and a toothpick inserted into the center comes out clean.

8. Let muffins rest in a pan on a wire rack for 5 minutes. Remove from the pan and let cool completely on the rack

Easy Chocolate Chip Muffins

Coffee and tea go better with chocolate!

Serving Size: 12 Muffins

Ingredients:

2 cups all-purpose flour
1 teaspoon baking powder
½ teaspoon baking soda
½ teaspoon salt
½ cup melted vegan butter
½ cup of sugar
½ cup packed light brown sugar
1½ teaspoons vanilla extract
1 tablespoon psyllium husk
1 cup sour cream room temperature
⅔ cup vegan mini chocolate chips, plus about 3 tablespoons more for sprinkling on top
1½ tablespoons coarse sugar for sprinkling on top

Instructions:

1. Preheat the oven to 350ºF and spray the muffin pan with oil spray.

2. In a mixing bowl, combine and whisk together the flour, baking powder, baking soda, and salt.

3. In a large bowl, whisk together the melted butter, granulated sugar, brown sugar, psyllium husk, and vanilla. Then, add the sour cream. Add the dry ingredients and whisk until evenly combined. Stir in ⅔ cup of the chocolate chips.

4. Spoon the batter evenly inside muffin cups filling ¾ full. Add a few chocolate chips to the tops from the remaining chocolate chips, followed by the coarse sugar.

5. Bake for 18 to 20 minutes, until golden brown.

6. Let the muffins cool in the pan for about 10 minutes, then transfer to a cooling rack.

Grandma's Banana Nut Muffins

These bad boys are a crowd favorite. We can't keep enough in stock because they fly off the shelf. Now you have the secret to keeping your tummy happy!

Serving Size: 12 Muffins

Ingredients:

1 cup all-purpose flour

½ cup whole wheat flour

1½ teaspoons baking soda

¼ teaspoon salt

½ cup melted butter

3 large ripe bananas mashed

½ cup of sugar

¼ cup dark brown sugar packed

¼ cup plant milk

1 tablespoon psyllium husk

1 teaspoon vanilla extract

¾ cup to 1 cup walnuts

Instructions:

1. Preheat the oven to 350°F.

2. Whisk the dry ingredients—flour, baking soda, and salt together in a large mixing bowl. Set aside.

3. Melt butter. Set aside.

4. In a separate mixing bowl, mash bananas with a fork. Mix in butter, both sugars, plant milk, psyllium husk, and vanilla. Stir until well combined.

5. Combine wet ingredients into dry ingredients. Stir until just combined. (Tip: Do not over mix). Fold in half the walnuts.

6. Spoon batter evenly into 12 greased muffin cups and sprinkle the remainder of walnuts over top of the muffins.

7. Bake for about 22 - 26 minutes or until muffins are golden brown and a toothpick inserted into the center comes out clean.

8. Let muffins rest in a pan on a wire rack for 5 minutes. Remove from the pan and let cool completely on the rack.

Espresso Double Chocolate Chip Muffins

Chocolate and Espresso. The ultimate dynamic duo!

Serving Size: 12 Muffins

Ingredients:

2 cups all-purpose flour

¾ cup unsweetened cocoa powder

2½ teaspoons baking powder

½ teaspoon baking soda

½ teaspoon salt

1¼ cups sugar

1 tablespoon psyllium husk

1¼ cups vegan buttermilk

¼ cup vegan butter melted and cooled

¼ cup oil

2 teaspoons espresso powder

1 teaspoon vanilla extract

1 cup mix of vegan chocolate chips and chunks

Instructions:

1. Preheat oven to 425℉ degrees.

2. Grease 12 muffin cups.

3. Melt the butter in a medium saucepan on the stovetop, and let it cool a bit while you prepare the other ingredients.

4. In a large bowl, sift the dry ingredients together flour, cocoa, baking powder, baking soda, and salt. Add sugar and mix. Set aside.

5. In a medium bowl, whisk the psyllium husk with the buttermilk, oil, melted butter, instant coffee, and vanilla extract.

6. Pour the wet ingredients into the dry ingredients and stir with a wooden spoon until combined. Do not over mix. (Tip: The batter should be lumpy)

7. Add chocolate chips/chunks and stir.

Recipe Continued on Next Page

Espresso Double Chocolate Chip Muffins Continued

8. Spoon batter evenly between the muffin cups and fill them almost to the top.

9. Bake for 3 minutes and then reduce the oven temperature to 350°F.

10. Continue to bake for an additional 12-17 minutes (15-20 minutes total) until a toothpick inserted into the center of the muffin comes out clean.

11. Place on the counter to cool. Remove out of the muffin pan after 10 minutes

COACH MIKA

Seek Inner Growth and there you will find joy

Mika wears many hats. Not only is she a chef, but she is also a certified life coach who is a leading expert in self-esteem and peak performance.

<u>Apple Bread</u>

Slice and serve with your favorite vegan ice cream or whipped cream!

Serving Size: 8 Slices

Ingredients:

1½ cups all-purpose flour
½ cup brown sugar packed
1½ teaspoons cinnamon
½ cup sugar
½ cup vegan butter (1 stick) softened to room temp
2 large cut peeled puréed apples
2 teaspoons vanilla extract
1½ teaspoons baking powder
1 cup plant milk
1 teaspoon psyllium husk
¼ teaspoon salt
1¼ cup peeled and chopped apples (into 2-inch chunks) about 2 small apples

Instructions:

1. Preheat the oven to 350℉ degrees. Spray a large loaf pan with nonstick cooking spray or grease with vegan butter or oil.

2. In a bowl, mix together brown sugar and cinnamon. Set aside

3. Using a stand mixer (or in a large bowl with an electric mixer), mix together sugar and butter until smooth.

4. Purée apples in a blender.

5. Stir puréed apples and vanilla extract into the large mixing bowl until fully combined.

6. Finally, stir in flour, salt, psyllium husk, and baking powder, and plant milk. Mix until combined.

7. Pour half the batter into the prepared loaf pan.

8. Cover batter with half the diced apples. Press the apples down slightly into the batter.

9. Sprinkle the apples with half the cinnamon-sugar mixture.

Continued on Next Page

Apple Bread Continued from the previous page

10. Pour the remaining batter over the apple layer.

11. Decorate with remaining diced apples on top.

12. Sprinkle the remaining cinnamon-sugar mixture on top.

13. Bake in the center rack for about 40-46 minutes. (Tip: Until a toothpick inserted comes out clean.)

14. Allow to cool completely before removing from the baking pan.

Donations were made to many of the wonderful photographers on Pixel who provided artwork for our project.

Chocolate Chip Cookies

If you are anything like us, we gobble these down so quickly we have to have a stockpile for when friends and family pop in for a visit. These cookies are freezer-friendly. Just wrap them in foil and securely place them in a resealable bag, and they are ready to freeze for up to six months. When you crave these bad boys' sweet comfort, pull them out of the freezer and let them defrost. Better yet, after they defrost, microwave them for ten seconds, and they taste like they just came out of the oven.

Serving Size: 40-48 Cookies

Ingredients:

2½ cups flour

1 teaspoon baking powder

1 teaspoon baking soda

¼ teaspoon salt

⅓ cup of sugar

½ cup brown sugar

⅔ cup oil

2 teaspoons vanilla

¼ cup + 2 tablespoons plant milk

2 cups vegan chocolate chips

Instructions:

1. Preheat oven to 375℉.

2. In a large bowl, combine all ingredients (except chocolate chips) and mix with a wooden spoon until a smooth cookie dough forms. If the dough is too dry, add a tablespoon of plant milk.

3. Fold in the chocolate chips.

4. Line the cookie tray with parchment paper.

5. Use an ice cream scoop to form each round ball.

6. Place on a cookie tray about 2 inches apart.

7. Bake for 8-10 minutes or until the edges are lightly golden brown. (Tip: They will appear doughy, but that's what we want so that they are not over baked)

8. Let cool on the counter for 2 minutes before removing from the cookie tray.

○●○●○●○●○●○●○●○●○●○●○

Oatmeal Raisin Cookies

Grab a tall glass, and pour yourself some cold plant milk. Sit back, relax, and dunk away!

Serving Size: 20 Cookies

Ingredients:

½ cup vegan butter
½ cup brown sugar
½ cup white sugar
¼ cup plant milk
¼ teaspoon vanilla
1½ cups all-purpose flour
½ cup oats
1 teaspoon baking soda
1 teaspoon baking powder
½ cup raisins
½ cup oat bran

Instructions:

1. Preheat oven to 375℉.

2. Combine all ingredients (except oat bran) in a large mixing bowl with a wooden spoon to form a soft cookie dough. If the dough seems too dry, add ⅛ cup of plant milk at a time until you have the consistency desired.

3. Fold oat bran into the cookie dough.

4. Line the cookie tray with parchment paper.

5. Use an ice cream scoop to form each round ball.

6. Place the balls about 2 inches apart. Flatten to form cookie shapes and top with more raisins if desired.

7. Bake for 8-11 minutes or until the edges are a light golden brown. (Tip: They will appear doughy, but that is what we want so that they are not over baked)

8. Let cool on the counter for 2 minutes before removing from the cookie tray.

Better Peanut Butter Cookies

Absolutely irresistible! Creamy, crunchy, and sweet, add them to your next cookie tray.

Serving Size: 12 Cookies

°●○°*◇*◆*◇*°●°

Ingredients:

1 cup peanut butter
½ cup all-purpose flour
¼ cup brown sugar
¼ cup of sugar
1 teaspoon baking powder
1 teaspoon vanilla
½ salt

Instructions:

1. Preheat the oven to 350ºF.

2. In a large bowl, combine all ingredients and mix with a spoon. A soft dough will form.

3. With hands or dough cutter, cut dough into large 12 balls. Place each on a cookie tray lined with parchment paper.

4. Flatten each cookie gently and make a fork import on top of cookies.

5. Bake for 15 minutes or until the edges are golden brown.

6. Remove from the oven and let cool for 30 minutes before taking them out of the pan because they'll need time to firm up as they cool. (Tip: Don't skip this step)

Almond Butter White Chocolate Cookies

Add these babies to your holiday cookie tray. Be prepared for everyone to ask for the recipe.

Serving Size: 12 Cookies

Ingredients:

1 cup almond butter
½ cup all-purpose flour
½ cup vegan white chocolate chips
½ chopped macadamia nuts (optional)
1 cup sugar
1 teaspoon baking powder
1 teaspoon vanilla
½ salt

Instructions:

1. Preheat the oven to 350ºF.

2. In a large bowl, combine all ingredients and mix with a spoon.

3. Roll dough into 12 balls, place on a cookie tray lined with parchment paper.

4. Flatten each cookie gently and top with additional white chocolate chips and macadamia nuts.

5. Bake for 15 minutes or until the edges are golden brown.

6. Remove from the oven and let cool for 30 minutes before taking them out of the pan because they will need time to firm up as they cool.

Musings on the Perfect Brownie

Customers always ask me, "How did you get into baking?" I smile and think, *What a long and winding road my baking story has been.*

I am the proud daughter of Haitian immigrants. My mama can whip up Haitian dishes that embody the simple yet complex flavors of her homeland. While my roots are firmly founded in the tapestry of creole cooking, I was drawn to the comforts of "American" food. As a child, nothing spoke to my soul, more than hotdogs dripping in chili and cheese, hamburgers that were smoldering right off the grill, and french fries. Don't get me started on french fries. I spent years searching for the perfect fry. You know the one—deep-fried, golden and crispy on the outside, and oh-so-fluffy on the inside. However, to earn the coveted Best French Fry award, it needed to achieve salt dusting perfection. When I was a teenager, I would sneak off to get a taste of these American staples. It felt liberating to be able to indulge in what the purveyors of American comfort food offered. The indulgence of true American comfort food felt liberating.

At eighteen, I become untethered. I was the first person in my family to graduate from college. This independent exercise in spreading my wings brought me closer to my love affair with all varieties of American fare. With my most acute ability to remember my culinary awakening, I paint the picture of when I first met Betty.

Ms. Betty—you may know her as Betty Crocker—became a symbol of decadent freedom for me. As I peeled open my first box of chocolate fudge brownie mix, I knew I would never look back. I clearly remember the surge of euphoria overtaking my soul as I mixed the golden canola oil into the mound of cocoa infused dust. Taking the first bite of my very own version of Ms. Betty's brownies was the definitive moment I knew I was meant to deliver sweetness to whoever would accept.

To say this became an obsession is an understatement. I experimented with different variations on Ms. Betty's classic recipe. And then I promptly wrapped these brownies up in saran-wrap and delivered them to my neighbors. The recipients of my labor of love all had one thing in common: the expression of joy. Inevitably, their eyes widened as they accepted my offering. I relished their fervor as they licked the crumbs of chocolate off their plates. Their joy was my joy.

I embraced this gift and cultivated the art of baking. When I met Victor, he was immediately struck by my culinary passions. And as I grew in my health journey, I knew I needed to enhance this gift by infusing a vegan-spin on Ms. Betty's original masterpieces.

Much Love to You,

Mika

○●○●○●○●○●○●○●○●○●○●○●●○●●○●

Fudgiest Brownies

If chocolate is your thing, then these treats are heaven.

Serving Size: 16 Treats

Ingredients:

1½ cups plant milk

1 cup vegan chocolate chips

1⅔ cups all-purpose flour

1 teaspoon apple cider or white vinegar

1 teaspoon baking powder

½ teaspoon baking soda

¼ teaspoon salt

⅓ cup cocoa powder

¾ cup sugar

⅓ cup oil

1 teaspoon vanilla

1 teaspoon instant coffee

Instructions:

1. Preheat the oven to 350°F.

2. Line a 9x9 baking pan with parchment.

3. Create your vegan buttermilk by combining 1 cup of plant milk and apple cider. Mix and set aside.

4. In a medium saucepan on medium heat on the stovetop, add oil and vegan chocolate chips. Whisk the mixture on the stovetop and remove it from heat as chocolates begin to melt. Continue whisking until the melted chocolate is cool. Set aside.

5. Combine all wet ingredients into the vegan buttermilk mixing bowl. Add the melted chocolate and whisk all ingredients vigorously until well incorporated.

6. Combine all dry ingredients into a separate mixing bowl and whisk. Combine dry ingredients into the wet ingredients bowl, and whisk until smooth.

7. Transfer batter to prepared baking pan and smooth batter evenly in pan. Bake in the middle rack for 20-22 minutes or until the center of the brownie pan no longer jiggles. Remember, toothpicks can still show pieces of fudge. (Tip: Avoid over baking)

Blondie

Just like the famous singer, this Blondie packs a punch and harmonizes your taste buds with a power-packed range of flavors and textures.

Serving Size: 16 Bars

Ingredients:

1 cup cashew butter
2 cups packed brown sugar
1 cup plant milk
2 teaspoons vanilla extract
½ cup chopped macadamia nuts (optional)
½ cup white chocolate chips
1¾ cups all-purpose flour
½ teaspoon baking powder
½ teaspoon salt

Instructions:

1. Preheat the oven to 350°F degrees and spray a 9x9 pan with cooking spray or grease with oil.

2. In a large bowl, mix cashew butter and brown sugar. Add in the plant milk and vanilla and whisk vigorously until smooth.

3. Add the flour, baking powder, and salt and whisk until well combined.

4. Pour the batter into the prepared pan and smooth out.

5. Place in the oven to bake for 30 minutes until the edges are golden and the toothpick comes out mostly clean. Remove from the oven once the edges are lightly golden.

6. Allow to cool completely for about 30 minutes, then cut into squares.

Brookie

Yum! Yum! Yum! Layers of yum!

Serving Size: 24 Treats

Ingredients:

Brownie layer: Refer to The Fudgiest Brownie recipe above

Cookie layer: Refer to Chocolate Chip Cookie recipe

Instructions:

1. Preheat the oven to 350ºF.

2. In a parchment paper lined 9x13 pan, add the layer of brownie batter and spread evenly.

3. Drop spoonfuls of cookie dough over the entire brownie batter.

4. Bake for 20-24 minutes or until the edges begin to set.

5. Remove from the oven once baked and cool completely before slicing for easier cutting.

PB & J Blondie

Time to Sing-along: Peanut, Peanut Butter—and Jelly! Peanut, Peanut Butter and— jelly!

Then you take your blondie, and you eat it, you, eat it!

Serving Size: 16 Treats

Ingredients:
Blondie: Refer to Blondie recipe
1 cup of peanut butter
1 cup of jelly or jam

Instructions:

1. Preheat the oven to 350°F.

2. In a parchment paper-lined 9x9 pan, add the layer of blondie batter and spread evenly.

3. Drop spoonfuls of peanut butter and jelly over the entire blondie batter.

4. With a toothpick or small knife, make swirls on the surface of the batter.

5. Bake for 20-22 minutes or until the edges begin to set.

6. Remove from the oven once baked and cool completely before slicing for easier cutting.

Classic Baked Cheesecake

Need a dessert for your next party? Give this creamy classic a try.

Serving Size: 8 Slices

Ingredients:

Crust:

Follow the Flaky Pie Crust recipe

Filling:

⅓ cup cornstarch

½ cup sugar

1 can full-fat coconut milk

½ vegan evaporated milk

¼ teaspoon Himalayan salt

2 tablespoons vegan butter at room temperature

1 ½ teaspoon vanilla extract

Bananas:

slice 2 to 3 bananas

Topping:

Coconut Whip Cream

Instructions:

1. Pre-bake the Flaky Pie Crust, then let it cool while making the filling.

2. In a medium saucepan over medium heat, combine all ingredients (except butter and vanilla extract) and whisk continuously, bring to a boil. Boil for 4-5 minutes, then reduce to low heat. Use a rubber spatula to clean the sides and bottom of the pan. Continuously whisk for 1-3 minutes until it appears like a jiggly pudding.

3. Remove from heat. Stir in butter and vanilla extract.

4. Slice two bananas and place some on the bottom of the pie crust. Pour mixture into pie crust halfway. Add sliced bananas on top of the mixture. Pour the remaining custard into the pie crust.

5. Leave at room temperature for 10 minutes to cool. Cover with plastic wrap or eco-friendly alternatives such as 4MyEarth wrap. Wrapping will prevent a film from forming on top. (Tip: You don't want to skip this step.)

6. Refrigerate 3-4 hours or overnight.

7. Once chilled, spread coconut whip cream generously and evenly. Slice the third banana and decorate the pie right before serving. Serve before bananas turn brown.

○ ● ○ ● ○ ● ○ ● ○ ● ○ ● ○ ● ○ ● ○ ● ○ ● ○ ● ●

Mama's Coconut Cream Pie

My Haitian mother used coconut religiously in both sweet and savory dishes. She was even so kind as to feed us slices of coconut as we eagerly waited on standby in the kitchen.

Serving Size: 8 Slices

Ingredients:

Ingredients:

Crust:

See crust recipe from Classic Baked Cheesecake

Filling:

¼ cup cornstarch

⅔ cup sugar

1 can coconut cream

1 can coconut milk

¼ teaspoon Himalayan salt

1 cup shredded coconut from fresh or store-bought coconut

2 tablespoons vegan butter at room temperature

1 teaspoon vanilla extract

½ teaspoon coconut extract

Topping:

See Coconut Whipped Cream recipe.

Instructions:

1. Preheat the oven to 350°F.

2. Prebake pie crust in an 8-inch pie pan for 15-17 minutes or until edges are golden brown. Set aside.

3. In a medium saucepan over medium heat, combine all ingredients (except shredded coconut and coconut extract) and whisk continuously, bring to a boil. Boil for 4-5 minutes, then remove from heat. Stir in coconut extract and shredded coconut.

4. Pour warm filling into pie crust. Cover tightly with plastic wrap or eco-friendly wrap alternative like 4MyEarth brand food cover.

5. Refrigerate for at least 5 hours or overnight until thickened and chilled.

6. Follow the recipe for coconut whipped cream.

7. Remove the pie filling from the refrigerator. Once it has completely set, spread the coconut whipped cream on top of the filling and smooth. Sprinkle additional shredded coconut shavings on top of whipped cream to decorate.

8. Chill pie, and get ready to impress your in-laws or boss with this bomb coconut pie. (Tip: "Psst. Listen up" don't tell them it's vegan until the end)

Flaky Buttery Pie Crust

Many customers praise our vegan pies and wonder how we get them to taste so buttery and flaky. Lean in close, and we will tell you our secret. "It's in the crust."

Serving Size: One 9-inch Double Pie

Ingredients:

2½ cups all-purpose flour

1 teaspoon Himalayan salt

2 teaspoons brown sugar

1 cup very cold vegan butter (cut into ½ inch cubes)

5-8 tablespoons of ice water

Instructions:

1. Preheat oven to 375℉.

2. Add 1½ cups flour, brown sugar, and salt to a medium bowl. Stir 2 to 3 times until just combined.

3. Toss butter cubes over dry ingredients in the bowl and mix briefly with a fork or spatula to coat the butter with dry ingredients.

4. Working quickly—about 1-2 minutes to keep the butter cold—cut the butter into the dry ingredient with a dough scraper or pastry blender until the flour looks like a bread crumbs texture.

5. Add remaining 1 cup of flour. Continue cutting through butter and flour with the dough scraper or pastry blender until the flour is evenly distributed —about 20 seconds. The dough should look crumbly.

6. Sprinkle evenly about 4 tablespoons of ice water over the mixture. Add more if needed. Create a loose pie dough by using a rubber spatula, press the dough into itself. The crumbs should form larger clusters. If you pinch some of the dough and it holds together, it is ready. If the dough falls apart, add 2 to 4 more tablespoons of ice water and continue to press until the dough comes together.

7. Place dough on a clean surface, gently molding the dough just enough to form a ball. Cut the dough in half, then form each half into discs. Wrap each disc with plastic wrap and refrigerate for at least 1 hour and up to 2 days.

8. Allow one of the dough discs to sit at room temperature for 5 minutes.

Continued on next page

Flaky Pie Crust Continued from previous page

9. Sprinkle flour on the work surface, rolling pin, and the surface of the dough. On the dough disc, roll out a 12-inch circle (about 1/8-inch thick) using a rolling pin. Dust a little flour on the work area when needed to prevent dough from sticking to the table while rolling.

10. Place the pie pan or pie dish upside-down over the dough round. Look for a 1 inch excess around the pie dish. To transfer the dough to the pie dish, starting at one end, roll dough around the rolling pin, then unroll over the dish.

11. Gently press dough into the pie dish so that it lines the bottom and sides of the dish. Be careful not to stretch the dough. Then, use a knife or pair of kitchen shears to trim excess dough to within ½ inch of the edge of the dish.

12. Fold the excess edge of dough underneath itself so that it creates a thicker, 1/4-inch border that rests slightly over the pie dish. Then, crimp edges by pressing the pointer finger of one hand against the edge of the dough from the inside of the dish while gently pressing with two knuckles of the other hand from the outside. Refrigerate dough for at least 20 minutes or freeze for 5 minutes before baking. Freeze if not baking the same day up to three months in freezer wrap.

13. If making a double-crust pie, do not crimp edges yet. Roll out the second dough disc, fill the pie, then top with the second dough round. Trim the edges, then crimp.

14. With a fork, gently prick tiny holes all over the bottom of the dough to allow air to escape when the pie is baking.

15. Bake lined with parchment paper and pie weights or dry beans. Use aluminum foil or a pie shield to protect the crust edge from burning.

16. Reduce temperature to 350℉ and bake for 20 minutes. Remove parchment paper with pie. Pour pie filling and bake according to the pie's specifications. If using a no-bake pie recipe, bake the pie for an additional 20 minutes.

17. The crust should be a golden brown. Let cool before serving. Bon appetit!

Victor and Mika are known for their precision and innovation in creating over-the-top cakes that are works of art.

○●○●○●○○●○●○●○●○●○●○●○●○●○○●○●○

Old Fashioned Banana Cream Pie

Since childhood, I've been obsessed with banana desserts like banana bread, smoothies, ice creams, pies, and pudding. You get the picture. Welcome to my obsession.

Serving Size: 8 Slices

Ingredients:

Crust:

Follow the Flaky Pie Crust recipe

Filling:

⅓ cup cornstarch

½ cup sugar

1 can full-fat coconut milk

½ vegan evaporated milk

¼ teaspoon Himalayan salt

2 tablespoons vegan butter at room temperature

1½ teaspoons vanilla extract

Bananas:

slice 2 to 3 bananas

Topping:

Coconut Whip Cream

Instructions:

1. Pre-bake the Flaky Pie Crust, then let it cool while making the filling.

2. In a medium saucepan over medium heat, combine all ingredients (except butter and vanilla extract) and whisk continuously, bring to a boil. Boil for 4-5 minutes, then reduce to low heat. Use a rubber spatula to clean the sides and bottom of the pan. Continuously whisk for 1-3 minutes until it appears like a jiggly pudding.

3. Remove from heat. Stir in butter and vanilla extract.

4. Slice two bananas and place some on the bottom of the pie crust. Pour mixture into pie crust halfway. Add sliced bananas on top of the mixture. Pour the remaining custard into the pie crust.

5. Leave at room temperature for 10 minutes to cool. Cover with plastic wrap or eco-friendly alternatives such as 4MyEarth wrap. Wrapping will prevent a film from forming on top. (Tip: You don't want to skip this step.)

6. Refrigerate 3-4 hours or overnight.

7. Once chilled, spread coconut whip cream generously and evenly. Slice the third banana and decorate the pie right before serving. (Tip: Bananas can turn brown if not served immediately)

No-bake Oreo Cheesecake

"I didn't know Oreo cookies were vegan!" Is the typical response from our non-vegan clients, followed by a look of amazement and shock. Your friends and family will be equally shocked–in a good way– when you replicate this Oreo Cheesecake recipe.

Serving Size: 8 Slices

Ingredients:

Ingredients:

Crust:

25 Oreo cookies (both the wafers and fillings)

5 tablespoons vegan butter melted

Filling:

2 cup raw cashews, soaked for 20 minutes in hot water.

1 cup frozen Oreos

1 can coconut milk

½ cup agave

½ cup melted coconut oil

½ teaspoon Himalayan salt

Topping:

Chocolate ganache recipe

Instructions:

1. Pulse Oreos in the food processor until coarse crumbles are present, and add vegan butter. Or place Oreos in a ziplock bag and crush them with a rolling pin.

2. Press into the bottom and up the sides of a 9-inch spring pie pan, and then place in the freezer.

3. In a high-power blender, mix all the filling ingredients until well combined for 1 minute.

4. Using a rubber spatula to scrape the sides, pour the mixture onto the Oreo crust.

5. Place the pan in the freezer for 4 hours to set. Remove spring pan sides once the cheesecake is completely set, and place back in the freezer.

6. Slowly pour ganache on top of the warm cheesecake until you reach your desired coverage. (Tip: I like to let some drip down the sides of the cake). Your cheesecake won't melt because it is frozen.

7. Decorate the top of the cheesecake with more crushed Oreos or any other chocolates, nuts, or fruits you desire. Once you are satisfied with your presentation, place the cheesecake back in the freezer to allow the ganache to set.

8. Remove from the freezer 20 minutes before serving to give the cheesecake time to thaw.

Ooey-gooey Cinnamon Rolls

The nostalgic spicy smell fills our kitchen on Sunday mornings. My favorite tip for this recipe, "Go for it and use as much cream cheese icing as you want. It's your party, after all!"

Serving Size: 9 Rolls

Ingredients:

For the dough:

¾ cup warm milk

2¼ teaspoons yeast

¼ cup sugar

¼ cup vegan butter, melted

3 cups bread flour, plus more for dusting

¾ teaspoon salt

For the filling:

⅔ cup light or dark brown sugar

1½ tablespoons ground cinnamon

¼ cup vegan butter softened

For the cream cheese frosting:

½ teaspoon vanilla extract

3 tablespoons vegan butter, softened

¾ cup powdered sugar

4 ounces vegan cream cheese, softened

Instructions:

1. Warm plant milk on low heat for 3-5 minutes on the stovetop. Transfer warm milk to the bowl of an electric mixer and sprinkle yeast on top. Add in sugar and melted butter. Mix until well combined. Then add flour and salt, stirring with a wooden spoon until you see a dough forming.

2. Have your stand mixer with the dough hook attached and knead the dough on medium speed for 8 minutes. When you see dough becoming a smooth ball, and it is slightly sticky, it is ready. Add in 2 tablespoons more bread flour if it is too sticky. Knead the dough for 8-10 minutes on a well-floured surface. (Tip: If you prefer, use a stand mixer)

3. Place the dough ball into a pre-greased bowl, cover with a warm towel. Allow dough to rise for 1 hour to 1½ hours, or until doubled in size. This may take more or less time, depending on the humidity and temperature in your home.

4. Once dough doubles in size, remove from the bowl into a well-floured surface and roll out into a 14x9 inch rectangle. Spread softened butter over dough, leaving a ¼ inch margin at the edge of the dough.

Continued on next page

Ooey-gooey Cinnamon Rolls continued from the previous page

5. In a small bowl, add and mix brown sugar and cinnamon. Grab mixture and sprinkle over the buttered dough, then rub the brown sugar mixture into the butter.

6. Tightly roll the dough up, starting from the 9-inch side, and place the seam side down, making sure to seal the edges of the dough as best you can.

7. Cut into 1-inch sections with a serrated knife. You should get 9 large pieces.

8. Place parchment paper in a 9x9 baking pan. Put each cinnamon roll inside the pan, giving them just enough room to rise. Cover with a warm towel and rise for 30-45 minutes.

9. Preheat the oven to 350ºF. Remove towel and bake cinnamon rolls for 20-25 minutes or until just slightly golden brown on the edges. Allow them to cool for 5-10 minutes before frosting so that the inside is soft and gooey

Thank You to Krisie De Vera for many of our beautiful photos! To see more of her work, check out KDV Creates at www.kdvcreates.com

Yummy Pancakes

These decadent cakes are the perfect companion to your favorite vegan sausage.

Serving Size: 5 to 6 Pancakes

Ingredients:
1½ cups all-purpose flour
1 tablespoon baking powder
2 tablespoons sugar
1 tablespoon vinegar
¼ teaspoon salt
1 teaspoon vanilla
1 ½ cups plant milk
2 tablespoons oil
Syrup

Instructions:
1. Create buttermilk by whisking together plant milk and vinegar in a mixing bowl. Set aside.

2. Heat the non-stick skillet on medium heat.

3. Combine and gently whisk dry ingredients. Whisk in the wet ingredients, being careful not to over-mix. Set aside for 5 minutes.

4. Pour about ½ cup of batter into the skillet and cook over medium heat. Flip when the edges begin to dry and bubbles on the top start to pop.

5. Cook for another 1-2 minutes and serve with vegan butter and syrup. Instagram worthy!

○●○●○●○●○●○●○●○●○●○●○

Easy Blueberry Pancakes

Did you know that pancakes exist all over the world? They can be served for breakfast, brunch, lunch, or dinner, and each culture brings its unique flavor to them. Enjoy our vegan style pile of blueberry deliciousness!

Serving Size: 4 Pancakes

Ingredients:

1 cup blueberries

1½ cups all-purpose flour

1 tablespoon baking powder

½ teaspoon salt

2 tablespoons sugar

1 cup plant milk

½ cup water

¼ cup mashed banana

Instructions:

1. Whisk together the dry ingredients flour, baking powder, salt, and sugar in a large bowl.

2. In a separate bowl, whisk the wet ingredients milk, water, and oil. Add blueberries. Then pour into the dry ingredients bowl, and stir with a large wooden spoon until just combined. (Tip: Don't over mix)

3. Turn stove-top to medium-high under a large skillet. Grease the skillet with oil.

4. Once the skillet is hot, drop about ¼ cup of the batter onto it. Cook until bubbles form, then flip and cook until golden brown on the other side, about 1-2 minutes. Repeat with all the remaining batter.

5. Enjoy with your favorite syrup, vegan butter, and top with more blueberries.

○●○●○●○●○●○●○●○●○●○●○

Bakery Style Glazed Donuts

"Sometimes the table was graced with immense apple-pies, or saucers full of preserved peaches and pears; but it was always sure to boast of an enormous dish of balls of sweetened dough, fried in hog's fat, and called dough-nuts, or oly koeks: a delicious kind of cake, at present scarce known in this city, excepting in genuine Dutch families."

From Washington Irving's book: A History of New York, from the Beginning of the World to the End of the Dutch Dynasty. 1809

Serving Size: 12 Donuts and 12 Donut Holes

Ingredients:

Donuts

1 cup warm plant milk 110℉

⅓ cup sugar

1 package or 2¼ teaspoons active dry yeast

6 tablespoons softened vegan butter

1 teaspoon vanilla extract

¾ teaspoon salt

4 cups all-purpose flour (plus more if needed)

1-2 quarts of oil for frying

Glaze

2 cups of powdered sugar (confectioner's sugar)

1 teaspoon vanilla extract

⅓ cup of plant milk

Instructions:

1. In a mixing bowl, combine sugar, warm milk, yeast, and whisk for about 5 seconds. Let rest for 5 minutes. If it doesn't appear frothy, then the yeast is not activated, so you need to redo it with a new package of yeast.

2. Add the butter, vanilla, salt, and 2 cups of flour. With an electric mixer, beat on low speed for 1 minute with a stand mixer. Scrape down the sides of the bowl with a rubber spatula as needed. Add remaining flour and beat on medium speed until the dough comes together and pulls away from the sides of the bowl—about 2 minutes. If needed, add more flour, 1 tablespoon at a time, until the dough pulls away from the sides of the bowl. You don't want to add too much flour. The dough should be slightly sticky. (Tip: If you don't own an electric mixer, you can mix this dough with a large wooden spoon. It will take a bit of elbow grease!)

3. Knead the dough. Keep the dough in the mixer and beat for an additional 2 minutes or knead by hand on a lightly floured surface for 2 minutes.

Continued on Next Page

Bakery Style Glazed Donuts continued from previous page

4. Place the dough in a lightly oiled large mixing bowl. Cover with a warm, clean kitchen towel, and place in a warm area to rise uninterrupted 1-2 hours or until it has doubled in size.

5. When the dough has doubled, punch it down to release the air. Remove dough from the bowl and turn it out onto a lightly floured surface. If needed, punch down again to release any more air bubbles. Using a rolling pin, roll the dough out until it is ½ inch thick. Using a 3-3.5 inch doughnut cutter or a 3-inch glass cup, center with a 2 inch round cookie cutter and cut into 12 donuts. If you can't quite fit 12, re-roll the scraps to cut more.

6. Transfer the donuts to a parchment paper-lined baking sheet. Cover them with a warm kitchen towel and place the baking sheet in a warm spot to rise until puffy, about 1 hour.

7. While donuts have about 10 minutes left of rising, heat a large pot of oil to 375℉.

8. Once donuts have risen, place them on the counter. Prepare a rack with paper towels or cheesecloth to absorb the oil.

9. Place 2-3 doughnuts at a time in the oil to cook for 1 minute on each side.

10. Carefully remove each donut and place it on the prepared rack.

11. Repeat until all of the donuts are fried, then turn off the heat.

Glaze

Whisk all ingredients together. Dip each warm donut into the glaze while it's still hot. Coat both sides with the glaze. Place back onto the prepared rack as excess glaze drips down. After about 20 minutes, the glaze will set and harden.

FAMOUS VEGANS

ALEC BALDWIN, ARNOLD SCHWARZENEGGAR, MEGHAN MARKLE, MYLIE CYRUS, BRAD PITT, PAUL MCARTNEY, KATE MARA, J-LO, JAY-Z, BEYONCE, ELLEN DEGENERIS, ARIANA GRANDE

Plant-based diets are becoming more popular, as indicated by the many celebrities who are going green. In fact, in 2020, it was announced that the Oscars were offering entirely plant-based menus at the Oscar Nominees Luncheon and in the Dolby Theatre lobbies prior to the 92nd Academy Awards. The post-ceremony Governors Ball will be 70% plant-based and 30% vegetarian, fish, and meat. All food will be responsibly sourced and sustainably farmed.

Easy Diner Style Potatoes

The perfect side for any meal.

Serving Size: 8

Ingredients:

6 medium-sized potatoes

1 medium chopped onion

1 red bell pepper

1 green bell pepper

2 teaspoons minced garlic

¼ cup oil

¾ teaspoon smoked paprika

1 teaspoon salt

⅛ cup oil for frying

Instructions:

1. Heat a large skillet or pan over medium heat with oil.

2. In a large bowl, dice and combine the minced garlic, potatoes, smoked paprika, onions, bell peppers, oil, and salt. Toss until ingredients are coated in oil.

3. Add the vegetables to the skillet and stir and toss every 2 minutes to prevent sticking. Cook the potatoes for a total of 8-10 minutes.

4. Taste for seasonings and adjust to preference. Serve immediately with your favorite brunch entree!

Easy Tofu Scramble

Tofu absorbs flavors, and when prepared correctly, it can be quite savory.

Serving Size: 6

Ingredients:

1 block firm tofu drained

2 tablespoons nutritional yeast

1 tablespoon oil

½ teaspoon salt, or more to taste

¼ teaspoon turmeric

¼ teaspoon garlic powder

2 tablespoons unsweetened plant milk

½ cup favorite veggies

Instructions:

1. Over medium heat, heat a medium-sized skillet. Use hands to drain and crumble small and medium-sized pieces of firm tofu into the pan. Cook, frequently stirring, for 3-4 minutes until the water from the tofu is mostly gone.

2. Add nutritional yeast, salt, turmeric, and garlic powder. Cook and stir constantly for about 5 minutes.

3. Pour the plant milk into the skillet or pan and your favorite veggies like spinach, and stir to mix. Cook for 2 minutes. Enjoy!

Easy French Toast

If you want to raise your brunch or breakfast to the next level, serve with Syrup, powdered sugar, and fresh fruit.

Serving Size: 6 to 8 slices

Ingredients:

6-8 slices stale bread, preferably thick

1 cup unsweetened plant milk

¼ cup arrowroot powder

1 teaspoon ground flaxseeds

½ teaspoon baking powder

1 teaspoon ground cinnamon

2 teaspoons sugar

1 teaspoon vanilla

2-3 tablespoons of oil for frying

Instructions:

1. Add a little oil to the skillet or pan over medium-high heat.

2. In a large mixing bowl, whisk together the plant milk, arrowroot, ground flaxseeds, baking powder, cinnamon, sugar, and vanilla until well combined.

3. Soak each side of the bread in the batter and let soak for about 10 seconds, then add the bread to the pan and cook for 2-3 minutes on each side, until golden brown. Add more oil to the pan as needed in between pieces of bread if the pan is dry.

4. Serve with syrup, powdered sugar, and fresh fruit.

For these scrumptious treats delivered straight to your door visit Victory & Mika's Bakery website at: www.victormikabakery.square.site